Immigrants, the Bible, and You

CALVIN SHORTS

A series published by the Calvin Press
Titles in the Calvin Shorts Series:

Immigrants, the Bible, and You

Amanda W. Benckhuysen

CALVIN SHORTS

Grand Rapids, MI • calvin.edu/press

Published 2020 by The Calvin Press
3201 Burton St. SE
Grand Rapids, MI 49546

Publisher's Cataloging-in-Publication Data

Names: Benckhuysen, Amanda W, 1969-, author.
Title: Immigrants , the Bible , and you / Amanda W. Benckhuysen.
Series: Calvin Shorts.
Description: Includes bibliographical references. | Grand Rapid, MI: The Calvin Press, 2020.
Identifiers: LCCN 2020933997 | ISBN 978-1-937555-45-0 (pbk.) 978-1-937555-46-7 (ebook)
Subjects: LCSH Emigration and immigration--Biblical teaching. | Emigration and immigration--Religious aspects--Christianity. | Emigration and immigration--Moral and ethical aspects. | Social justice-- Religious aspects--Christianity. | Social ethics. | Christian ethics. | BISAC RELIGION / Biblical Studies / General | RELIGION / Christian Living / General | RELIGION / Christian Ministry / Discipleship | RELIGION / Christian Theology / Ethics | RELIGION / Religion, Politics & State | SOCIAL SCIENCE / Emigration & Immigration
Classification: LCC BS680.E38 .B45 2020| DDC 261.8/38--dc23

Cover design: Robert Alderink
Interior design and typeset: Katherine Lloyd, The DESK

Contents

Series Editor's Foreword

Midway along the journey of our life
I woke to find myself in some dark woods,
For I had wandered off from the straight path.

So begins *The Divine Comedy*, a classic meditation on the Christian life, written by Dante Alighieri in the fourteenth century.

Dante's three images—a journey, a dark forest, and a perplexed pilgrim—still feel familiar today, don't they?

We can readily imagine our own lives as a series of journeys: not just the big journey from birth to death, but also all the little trips from home to school, from school to job, from place to place, from old friends to new. In fact, we often feel we are simultaneously on multiple journeys that tug us in diverse and sometimes opposing directions. We recognize those dark woods from fairy tales and nightmares and the all-too-real conundrums that crowd our everyday lives. No wonder we frequently feel perplexed. We wake up shaking our heads, unsure if we know how to live wisely today or tomorrow or next week.

This series has in mind just such perplexed pilgrims. Each book invites you, the reader, to walk alongside experienced guides who will help you understand the contours of the road as well as the surrounding landscape. They will cut back the underbrush, untangle myths and misconceptions, and suggest ways to move forward.

And they will do it in books intended to be read in an evening or during a flight. Calvin Shorts are designed not just for perplexed pilgrims but also for busy ones. We live in a complex and changing world. We need nimble ways to acquire knowledge, skills, and wisdom. These books are one way to meet those needs.

John Calvin, after whom this series is named, recognized our pilgrim condition. "We are always on the road," he said, and although this road, this life, is full of perplexities, it is also "a gift of divine kindness which is not to be refused." Calvin Shorts takes as its starting point this claim that we are called to live well in a world that is both gift and challenge.

In *The Divine Comedy*, Dante's guide is Virgil, a wise but not omniscient mentor. So, too, the authors in the Calvin Shorts series don't pretend to know it all. They, like you and me, are pilgrims. And they invite us to walk with them as together we seek to live more faithfully in this world that belongs to God.

Susan M. Felch
Executive Editor
The Calvin Press

Additional Resources

In 2017, Pennylyn Dykstra-Pruim and Tim Baldwin gathered together a number of faculty, students, and alumni of Calvin University and Calvin Theological Seminary to form the Refugee and Immigration Collaborative. The Collaborative met periodically over the course of a year to study, discuss, and produce resources that would help Christians think about the issue of immigration from the perspective of faith. Among the resources the collaborative produced are a website (https://ri-collaborative .org/) with stories, short videos, and other helpful material and two companion volumes on immigration in the Calvin Shorts series:

Immigration Debates in America by William Katerberg
Immigrants, The Bible, and You by Amanda W.
  Benckhuysen

For those who seek to grow in their understanding of biblical perspectives, history, and current realities of immigration, we offer the fruit of our participation in the Collaborative as a good place to start.

Additional online resources, for *Immigrants, the Bible, and You,* including discussion questions, are available at www.calvin.edu/press. References and citations are included in the notes at the end of this book. Rather than using footnote numbers, the comments are keyed to phrases and page numbers.

Immigrants, the Bible, and You
is underwritten by Calvin Theological Seminary.

The Refugee and Immigration Collaborative was funded by the Calvin Center for Christian Scholarship and the Calvin Alumni Association.

Acknowledgments

This project originated with an invitation from Pennylyn Dykstra-Pruim and Tim Baldwin to participate in the Refugee and Immigration Collaborative at Calvin University. The Collaborative was a group of faculty, students, and alumni that met together over the course of a year to study and discuss issues of immigration from a perspective of faith. Much of the material in this book was introduced and honed during our time together. I'm so grateful for the friendship, support, and learning I experienced with and through this group. Many thanks to Pennylyn Dykstra-Pruim, Tim Baldwin, Sarah Yore-Van Oosterhout, Stacey Wieland, Michelle Lloyd-Paige, Kate Kooyman, Ahee Kim, Will Katerberg, Bill Garvelink, Elvis Garcia Callejas, and Anh Vu Sawyer for sharing your stories and enriching my thinking about the challenges of immigration. A big thanks also to Susan Buist for all her work in keeping us organized and well-fed during our meetings.

The Refugee and Immigration Collaborative was co-sponsored by the Calvin Center for Christian Scholarship and the Calvin Alumni Association. I am grateful for their support for this endeavor which has led to the production of this and other resources to help Christians think about immigration from the perspective of faith. Thank you also to Calvin Theological Seminary for their generous support of this book project through a Faculty Heritage Fund Grant. A huge thanks to Susan Felch for her expertise and excellent suggestions in making this book clearer and more readable. I couldn't have completed this project without her input and encouragement. And also to Michaela Osborne for her immense patience with me in the process of deciding various details about the book.

Finally, I'd like to thank my daughters Kiya and Syann, and my husband Martin, for their patience and support while writing this book. None of this would be possible without their encouragement.

In the end, my prayer is that the words of this book and the discussions they yield nurture in the church greater love for God and for others. To God be all the glory.

Current Realities and Ancient Wisdom

1

In September 2015, three-year-old Alan Kurdi drowned in the Mediterranean Sea as his family was fleeing violence in Syria. Photos of his small lifeless body, which had washed up on a Turkish beach, were circulated in newspapers and social media outlets around the world. For many, Alan Kurdi's death became a wake-up call to the misery and desperation of a growing number of those around the world who have been forced from their homes by war, violence, and persecution.

By the end of 2019, the United Nations counted over 70.8 million people who had been displaced from their homes. This is the largest number of displaced persons on record since World War II. Included in this number are refugees, internally displaced persons, and asylum seekers. Each of these groups is made up of people who have been forced from their homes because of a well-founded fear of persecution, conflict, or generalized violence that has seriously disrupted the public order. While these groups share much in common, there are important differences that are worth noting here.

Refugees are those who, in fleeing their home, have crossed an international border and whose well-founded fear has been formally recognized by a government or by the United Nations High Commissioner for Refugees

(UNHCR). Internally displaced persons are those who have fled their homes but have not crossed an international border to find safety. Asylum seekers are those who have fled their homes and who enter or seek to enter another country to apply for protection.

All displaced persons are migrants, that is, people who are on the move from one location to another. Migrants become immigrants when they move to a foreign country with the intention of living there permanently. There are a variety of reasons why immigrants move to a country that is not their own. Some move because of economic opportunities or because of a job. Others move to be closer to family or in pursuit of a better quality of life. Refugees and asylum seekers move because life in their own country is no longer possible. While this book deals with issues related to immigration as a whole, much of the focus is on refugees and asylum seekers who desire to make the United States their home.

Currently, there are 25.9 million people with refugee status, many who languish in United Nations–sponsored camps or in makeshift dwellings. Another 3.5 million asylum seekers are on the run, actively seeking a safe place to call home. The majority come from Syria, South Sudan, Afghanistan, Myanmar (Burma), and other parts of Africa and the Middle East. A growing number, many who are women and children, are fleeing unparalleled violence in El Salvador, Honduras, and Guatemala.

US RESPONSE TO THE REFUGEE CRISIS

Even as the number of people needing a new home continues to grow, the United States has been implementing policies designed to keep people out of this country. In 2017, for instance, the US government introduced an immigration ban on those from Muslim-majority countries. It set the ceiling for refugee resettlement for 2018 at a historic low of 45,000. And it implemented a controversial "zero-tolerance" policy, whereby asylum seekers who entered the country illegally were criminally prosecuted. This policy allowed officials to separate children from their parents at the border and detain them separately for weeks, sometimes months, after they arrived here. Government officials admitted that the goal of this policy was to discourage families from applying for asylum in the US.

The government officially ended the zero-tolerance policy in June 2018. However, family separations at the border continued. Approximately 5,500 immigrant children were separated from their parents between 2017 and 2019. Eleven hundred of these separations occurred after the policy of family separations officially ended.

Furthermore, since 2018, the government has continued to lower the ceiling for refugee resettlement. For 2019, the cap was set at 30,000, and for 2020, it was 18,000. To put this in perspective, between 1999 and 2016, the refugee ceiling ranged from 70,000 to 91,000. Until recently, the US was the world leader in refugee resettlement. Now

Canada has assumed this role. Over the last three years, the US has admitted only 76,200 refugees. By comparison, in 2016 alone, nearly 85,000 refugees were resettled in the US.

Myth #1:
America is being overrun with immigrants.

It is true that the actual number of immigrants living in the US is greater than ever before. However, the percentage of immigrants in the overall population is not much different than at other times in US history. Since the beginning of the 20th century, the immigrant population has comprised anywhere between 10-15% of the population. Currently, immigrants make up 13.6% of the population. This number includes all foreign-born naturalized citizens, visa and green card holders, and undocumented residents in the US.

Compared to the percentage of foreign-born residents in other developed countries, the US is on the low side. In Canada, New Zealand, Switzerland, and Australia, for instance, foreign-born residents make up more than 20% of the population.

It is also worth noting that the number of undocumented persons residing in the US is about 3.2% of the population. This number has seen a sharp decline in the last decade.

Some have suggested that the government is lowering the refugee ceiling to direct more resources to asylum seekers at our southern border. However, even while closing the door to refugees, the government continues to institute policies that deter or prevent asylum seekers from even reaching the border. For instance, in July 2019, government officials approved a policy that prevents immigrants from being granted asylum if they pass through another country before arriving in the US. This policy effectively disqualifies the majority of those heading for the US border from making a claim for asylum.

COMMON ATTITUDES ABOUT IMMIGRANTS

Pointing the finger at our current government for this unwelcoming posture toward immigrants would be convenient. Surveys indicate, however, that these protectionist measures reflect the attitudes of a significant portion of the American population. According to a 2018 survey, for instance, only 51 percent of Americans believe that the United States has a responsibility to accept refugees into the country, while 43 percent do not. Among white evangelical Christians, the number of those who say that the US has no responsibility toward refugees rises to 68 percent.

Behind these statistics lie deep concerns and fears about the changing demographic and color of America. According to a Public Religion Research Institute survey conducted in 2018, 37 percent of white Americans and 57 percent of white evangelical Christians believe that newcomers are a threat to traditional American customs and values. Americans fear what will become of their homeland if immigrants make up a growing percentage of the population. Because immigrants are perceived as a danger and a threat, Americans tend to support tight controls and restricted access to the US.

In some ways, this protectionist stance is understandable. It is natural to want to ensure the well-being of oneself and one's own. The question, however, is whether fear should be the first and the last word in the conversation about immigrants. Perhaps there are other considerations that should come into play.

For instance, does a nation rich in resources like our own have a moral responsibility to help those who are fleeing poverty and violence? Is "threat" the only or most accurate way to think about those who seek to enter the US? Do immigrants really take from America more than they give? Given the pressing nature of this crisis and the human lives at stake, it seems right that we should spend some time examining our attitudes toward immigrants more closely.

This seems especially important for those who are followers of Jesus Christ. As Christians, we take our cues for engaging with the world around us not from government officials or from the broader culture but from God. Thus, while we are called to submit to those in authority (Romans 13:1), our first allegiance is to God and his kingdom. We are in the world but not of it. When it comes to immigrants, then, our attitudes should reflect those who have the mind of Christ. They should be rooted in faith, not in fear.

BIBLICAL WISDOM ABOUT IMMIGRANTS

This book is an invitation to take some time to think deeply about immigrants in the context of faith. The main guide for this journey will be the Bible. For Christians, the Bible functions as a compass, orienting us to the ways and will of God. It teaches us not only the good news of the gospel of Jesus Christ but also how we are called to live in light of that gospel. In other words, it teaches us how to love God, how to live for God, and how to serve God.

With respect to immigrants, the Bible has quite a bit to say, showing us something of God's heart for those who lack a home and a community. In fact, over one hundred passages of Scripture take up the cause of the immigrant. Many of these passages urge Israel to treat the immigrant with justice and compassion. Others go further, commanding Israel to love the immigrant. A good example is Deuteronomy 10:18–19, where we read that God loves the immigrant, so we are to love the immigrant too.

*Do you want to read more of
what the Bible says about immigrants?*

Take the 40-day "I was a Stranger" challenge. The challenge will guide participants to read through relevant Bible passages and pray for immigrants for 40 days.

Go to: **www.evangelicalimmigrationtable
.com/#resources**

Of course, loving the immigrant does not mean throwing open our borders to let anybody and everybody in without limitations or restrictions. The Bible is not naive about the dangers or challenges that foreigners can pose to a community. Israel itself experienced occasions when foreigners inflicted harm. One has only to think of Jezebel, who refused to accept the laws of the land and the limits those laws placed on the king (1 Kings 21). The results were disastrous! The leaders of the community were led to engage in widespread deception, and an innocent life was lost. Still, what the authors of the Bible recognized is that just because some foreigners pose a threat, this does not mean that all do. To get at this distinction, they used different terms to distinguish between different types of foreigners.

For instance, in the Old Testament, the Hebrew word *zur* refers to things or people who are dangerous and seek to harm the community. *Zur* is frequently used to describe an invading or attacking army. Not surprisingly, Israel is permitted, even urged, to protect themselves against such foreigners.

A second term, *nekhar*, is used to describe a foreigner whose intentions are unknown. These might be people who dwell in the land but who are unwilling to commit themselves to Israel's welfare and join themselves to the community. This is not a term that is used often, but when the Old Testament describes a foreigner this way, it encourages caution.

So, for instance, Exodus 12:43 describes the regulations for the celebration of the Passover meal. The Israelites are told, "No foreigner [*nekhar*] may eat it [the Passover meal]." A few verses later, however, the text seems to change its tune. In verse 48, we read, "If an immigrant who lives with you wants to observe the Passover to the LORD, then he and all his males should be circumcised. Then he may join in observing it. He should be regarded as a native of the land." Is the Bible contradicting itself here? The answer is no. Rather, this verse is using a different Hebrew word, the word *ger*, for the English term "foreigner" or "immigrant."

In contrast to *zur* and *nekhar*, *ger* describes those who live among the Israelites and share their life with them. These are foreigners who have committed themselves to the well-being of Israel and have accepted its laws. A good example of this sort of foreigner is the Moabite Ruth. Ruth joins herself to her mother-in-law, Naomi, and becomes fully grafted into the people of God. In fact, as the Gospel of Matthew reminds us, God uses Ruth to play a key role in his plan of redemption. It is from her line that both King David and Jesus are born (1:5–6, 16). You could say that without Ruth, there would be no David and no Jesus. The majority of texts in the Bible are about these kinds of foreigners, immigrants who wanted to be part of Israel and who joined themselves to the people and their laws.

IMMIGRANTS, THE BIBLE, AND YOU

Most immigrants who want to settle in the United States are of this sort. They are people who are interested in making the US their home because they love America and what it stands for. In fact, they come here because they are attracted to the freedom and the opportunities that America holds for them and their children. Rather than seeking to destroy America, most immigrants are deeply committed to protecting and defending the democratic values on which this country was built. Furthermore, extensive security screening and background checks minimize the risk of admitting foreigners who intend to do harm.

For this reason, our exploration of biblical texts about immigrants will focus on the *ger*. As noted above, over one hundred passages take up the cause of the immigrant. Because it would be too much to survey each passage, the chapters that follow highlight key biblical themes that reflect the Bible's attitude toward the immigrant (*ger*).

Chapter 2 explores the story of Hagar in Genesis 16 as an illustration of God's heart for the immigrant. Chapter 3 focuses on human beings as image bearers of God and what this means for how we treat immigrants. Chapter 4 explores the vulnerability of immigrants and the laws God instituted to protect and care for them. Chapter 5 addresses the concerns about undocumented immigrants in light of Romans 13 and the biblical call to obey government authorities. Finally, chapter 6 explores what immigrants have to teach Christians about being strangers and foreigners in this world (1 Peter 2:11).

Discussion questions for each chapter and other resources are available at www.calvin.edu/press. These resources are designed to deepen the reader's understanding of and engagement with issues related to immigration. They will be especially helpful for those who want to read this book in a group setting. By the end of this book, readers will have a strong biblical foundation and a supply of practical wisdom for thinking about, interacting with, and advocating for immigrants today. It is to this task that we now turn our attention.

Immigrants and the God Who Sees

2

A good place to start exploring biblical perspectives on immigration is the story of Hagar in Genesis 16. Hagar is the Egyptian slave girl of Abram and Sarai. She left her homeland and came to Canaan not by her own choice but as the property of another. It is likely that she was part of the gift of sheep, cattle, donkeys, camels, and male and female slaves that the pharaoh gave to Abram when he took Sarai into his palace (Genesis 12:16). But Hagar is more than simply another article among Abram's acquired wealth. In Hebrew, the original language in which the Old Testament was written, Hagar's name sounds like the word for "the sojourner" or "the immigrant." Given the significance of names in the Old Testament, it seems likely that this is intentional and that the Bible is inviting us to read Hagar's story as the story of an immigrant.

Genesis 16 opens with the spotlight on Abram and Sarai and the problem of offspring. God had promised Abram a biological son (Genesis 15:4), but after ten years of living in Canaan, Abram and Sarai are no closer to having children. Sarai is still barren. So in line with common practices in the ancient Near East, Sarai asks Abram to sleep with her slave so she can have a child through Hagar. It is worth noting that Hagar has no say in the matter. She is simply a pawn in this scheme, given and taken without consent. Sarai's scheme works, and Hagar gets pregnant. Rather than solving the problem of offspring, however, Hagar's pregnancy complicates matters. Hagar is now enjoying the blessing and privilege that Sarai had so longed for. As Hagar's belly begins to swell with child, Sarai's heart fills with jealousy and Hagar's with a new awareness of her own significance. The relationship between master and slave has changed. To reassert her position and authority, Sarai abuses Hagar. In response, Hagar flees from the household into the wilderness.

What is striking about the biblical text at this juncture is that when Sarai and Hagar separate, the narrator's and, more significantly, God's attention follow Hagar. Though Abram and Sarai are the ones chosen to be the bearers of God's blessings and promises, in this moment, it is Hagar, the poor, black, immigrant slave girl, who captures God's attention, concern, and compassion. Hagar's testimony about God in Genesis 16:13 sums up her experience well: "You are El Roi [the God who sees]," she says. Perhaps for the first time in her life, Hagar feels that she has been seen, really seen, for who she is. God noticed her, acknowledged her, and attended to her. And it seems clear in the text that Hagar was deeply blessed by this interaction. The question this raises, of course, is What did God see when he looked at Hagar? As we read the text closely, a number of important qualities about this poor Egyptian foreigner and immigrant stand out.

WHAT GOD SEES IN HAGAR

The first thing to notice is that God sees Hagar as more than just the labels that Abram and Sarai use to describe her. Throughout the narrative, in their direct speech to each other and to Hagar, Abram and Sarai never refer to Hagar by name. She is always spoken of as the Egyptian slave girl. The impression one gets is that Hagar was never addressed by her name in the household of Abram and Sarai. Instead, she was objectified and identified only by her role and status.

By contrast, when the messenger of the Lord encounters Hagar, the first thing he does is call her by her name . . . Hagar. It is a simple act but a profound one, whereby the messenger of the Lord acknowledges that Hagar is not just an Egyptian immigrant or a slave but a human being. Hagar is a person with a name, an identity, and a story. When God looks at Hagar, then, he sees first of all an image bearer of God, one who has been endowed by her Creator with dignity and value and worth.

Second, God sees and acknowledges the way that Hagar has been mistreated by Abram and Sarai. "Where did you come from and where are you going?" the messenger of the Lord asked. "From Sarai my mistress. I'm running away," Hagar replied. And the angel of the Lord said to her, "Go back to your mistress. Put up with her harsh treatment of you" (Genesis 16:8–9). The word for "harsh treatment" here is the same word that is used earlier in the narrative to describe Sarai's treatment of Hagar. It is also the word used later in Exodus to describe the Egyptians' treatment of the Israelites before they cried out to God and he delivered them. By using the term "harsh treatment," the messenger acknowledges Hagar's hardship. She has been treated badly in ways that are dehumanizing. She is right to want to flee this oppressive situation. This is not what God intended for human beings, and Hagar is right to want more.

Myth #2:
Immigrants bring crime and violence to America

Actually, statistics suggest that the crime rate among immigrants is as much as 40% lower than that of the general population. This suggests that immigrants are less likely to commit crimes than native-born Americans. In fact, from 1990-2010 when the number of undocumented persons in the US was increasing, the violent crime rate and property crime rate in the US dropped significantly.

Additionally, there is little evidence to suggest that immigrants are more likely to be linked to terrorist organizations. Instead, the vast majority of those linked to terrorist incidents since 2002 are US citizens.

Some may wonder why God would send Hagar back to Abram and Sarai when he knows that she will be returning to an oppressive situation. This seems cruel and uncaring. While we cannot know with certainty God's motivations,

Hagar's multiple experiences with God suggest a relationship of care and compassion rather than cruelty.

One possibility may be that there were simply no good options for Hagar. She was, after all, a poor, black, pregnant woman alone in the wilderness without any resources. The chances of her and her unborn child surviving in these circumstances were not high. The wilderness was not a hospitable place for a pregnant woman. Remaining there would put her at risk for dehydration, starvation, exposure to the elements, kidnapping, rape, and being trafficked, robbed, or murdered. Returning to Abram and Sarai was certainly a hardship. Still, it held out the possibility for survival for both Hagar and her son. And perhaps that is what is behind God's command to Hagar. Her survival. How striking that God is committed to safeguarding the lives of Hagar and her child, particularly given the fact that neither Hagar nor her son will play a role in God's redemptive purposes in the future. God simply acts out of love and concern for this marginalized, oppressed, vulnerable woman and her son.

Finally, as God looks upon Hagar in the wilderness, he sees someone who has a contribution to make to the world. Like every image bearer of God, Hagar is full of potential. Thus, when God sees Hagar, this poor, single, unwed, pregnant woman who needs water, food, lodging, and protection, he looks beyond her immediate need and sees her not as a drain on Abram's household but rather as what she will become by God's grace. "I will give you many children, so many they can't be counted!" (Genesis 16:10).

Hagar will become a great nation. By God's promise and with God's blessing, Hagar, like Abram and Sarai, will be fruitful and multiply and live out the commission in Genesis 1:28 to fill the earth and care for it.

Loving our Muslim Neighbor

God promises Abraham that he will become a great nation through Isaac. Strikingly, God makes the same promise to Hagar. Through Ishmael, she would have many progeny.

Just as the Jews trace their ancestry back to Abraham through Isaac, several prominent Arab tribes trace their line back to Abraham through Ishmael. One prominent descendant in Ishmael's line is Muhammad, the founder and esteemed prophet of Islam.

In both Genesis 16 and 21, we read of God's great love and care for Hagar and Ishmael which ensured their survival. This raises an important question for us: What does God's love and care for Hagar and Ishmael mean for how we think about and interact with those who are followers of Islam? How might God's attitude toward Hagar and Ishmael help shape our own attitudes toward Muslims?

CALLED TO LOVE

It is striking how closely the promise made to Hagar resembles the one made to Abram and Sarai. What distinguishes

Abram and Sarai from Hagar, then, is not primarily God's blessing or God's love or God's attention but rather God's calling. Abram and Sarai are specifically called by God to participate in his redemptive work in the world. In Christian circles, "election" has often been understood in terms of salvation. God elects people, chooses them, to receive the gift of faith that leads to salvation. However, in Genesis 12:1–3, God chooses Abram and Sarai not just for salvation but to be the family through whom God will work out his purposes to redeem his world. Abram, Sarai, and their progeny are called to participate in God's redemptive work by being a blessing to the nations.

Unfortunately, Abram and Sarai are anything but a blessing to Hagar. They miss the opportunity to live out God's calling to participate in his redemptive mission in their relationship with Hagar, choosing instead to participate in her suffering. God, then, does what Abram and Sarai fail to do. God sees Hagar and acknowledges her personhood, her suffering, and her potential. She too is an image bearer of God with inherent dignity and worth. And so, on Hagar, God lavishes his attention, compassion, and love.

In the next few chapters, we will look more closely at these themes both as we find them in Scripture and as they pertain to the question of immigrants today. One important takeaway from this chapter, however, is how big and high and deep and wide God's love is. It isn't limited to certain people groups based on ethnicity, socioeconomic status, or gender. God's love and care are not even limited to those who love and worship him. Instead, God's love knows no bounds. He desires for all people to be reconciled to him. God invites us, like Abram and Sarai, to participate in this great, expansive love for the world and for all people. Like Abram and Sarai, we the church are called particularly for this task, to be ambassadors of God's love and grace here on earth. The only question is Will we join with God in loving and caring for those like Hagar?

Immigrants as
Image Bearers
of God

3

As we explored in the previous chapter, Hagar's story gives us some insight into how God sees immigrants. Among the things God saw as he looked upon Hagar was that she was a human being. While Abram and Sarai highlighted the differences between Hagar and themselves, God recognized their common humanity. Like Abram and Sarai, Hagar too was a person with a name, an identity, and a story.

The significance of Hagar's humanity cannot be overstated. According to Scripture, to be a human being is to bear the image of God. "God created humanity in God's own image, in the divine image God created them, male and female God created them" (Genesis 1:27). What this means exactly has been the topic of much conversation among biblical scholars and theologians alike. According to traditional interpretations of this text, human beings image God in three ways: their ability to reason, their ability to choose right from wrong, and their ability to be in relationship with God. In theological circles, these qualities have traditionally been considered unique attributes of human beings. They define what it means to be human in comparison to the rest of the created order.

BEARING GOD'S IMAGE

While this interpretation has appeal and is not entirely wrong, biblical scholars have suggested another way to think about what it means to bear God's image. In the ancient world, it was believed that the king represented the nation's supreme god to the people. He ruled according to the divine mandate of the nation's god. The language used to describe this relationship was that of imaging. The king was said to bear the image of god. Within the ancient world, then, imaging god was closely associated with authority, power, responsibility, and rule. Drawing on this concept, the author of Genesis attributes the image of God not just to kings but to all human beings. In Genesis, all human beings are to rule over the created order. All human beings share in the task of imaging God's reign here on earth.

The specific words used to describe this commission in Genesis 1 are found in verse 28. Human beings are to be fruitful and multiply, fill the earth and rule over it. In the Reformed tradition of Christianity, this commission is often referred to as the cultural mandate. The point here is not that human beings are to lord it over the natural world. Rather, they are given the responsibility and the opportunity to develop the potential of the world God created. They are to cultivate it and tend to its flourishing.

As image bearers of God, we are born with a natural impulse to want to produce and to contribute something meaningful to this world. We see this in our desire to have children. We also see it in our attempts to extend, expand, and enrich the world with our own unique offerings. We might call this activity culture-making. When we consider immigrants as imager bearers in this way, several implications immediately surface.

HUMAN DIGNITY AND WORTH

First, whatever honor, respect, and dignity were given a king as an image bearer of the nation's god, the author of Genesis now attributes to all human beings. All human beings are worthy of our respect and attention. All human beings have an inherent dignity and worth. All human beings share in the honor of representing God, bearing God's image here on earth. This continues to be true even though human beings disobeyed God and introduced sin into the world. We see this in the testimony of the psalmist, who, in the context of a sinful world, declares that human beings are created a little lower than the heavenly beings and crowned with glory and honor (Psalm 8:5). So while the image of God in us may be tarnished by sin, the Scripture writers insist that it has not been lost or taken away. We continue to bear God's image today.

This is not simply a theoretical concept. The fact that all human beings have inherent dignity and worth has practical implications. It affects how we think about others. How we structure our society. How we live in community with one another. One widely accepted implication of human dignity and worth is that all human beings are entitled to basic rights and freedoms.

The exact connection between human dignity and basic human rights continues to be a matter of debate among philosophers and theologians alike. However, the association itself has become commonly accepted. In fact, this notion formed the basis for the Universal Declaration of Human Rights (UDHR) adopted by the United Nations General Assembly in 1948. The declaration identifies a common standard of human rights to which all people are entitled because of their inherent dignity and worth. Among other things, these basic human rights include the right to life and liberty, the right to freedom from slavery and torture, and the right to work and to have an education.

So what does all this mean for immigrants and, in particular, refugees and asylum seekers? At the very least, it suggests that the global community has a collective moral responsibility to those fleeing danger. In other words, we have an obligation to participate in promoting and protecting their basic human rights. Again, the UN is particularly helpful here, uniting the international community around some key policies and practices regarding refugees and asylum seekers.

We find these policies and practices detailed in the 1951 Refugee Convention and the 1967 Protocol Relating to the Status of Refugees. These state that countries may not forcibly return refugees to a territory where they face danger. Countries may not discriminate between groups of refugees. Countries should not impose penalties on refugees or asylum seekers for illegal entry into their country provided they present themselves without delay to the authorities. Countries should ensure that refugees and asylum seekers receive the same rights and basic help as any other foreigner who is a legal resident, including access to medical care, schooling, public assistance, and the right to work. And countries should allow a spouse or dependent children to join persons to whom temporary refuge or asylum has been granted.

These UN-backed protocols are a good place to start as we think about the practical implications of the human dignity and worth of refugees and asylum seekers. As Christians who believe that human beings are image bearers of God, we should be particularly energetic in promoting these rights for refugees and asylum seekers in our country and in our communities.

HUMAN POTENTIAL

A second implication of being divine image bearers is that all people have unique gifts, talents, interests, and passions that they can use to develop the potential of God's good creation. Like Hagar, we all have the potential to contribute something positive to the world. This is no less true of immigrants. Immigrants all have gifts with which to bless their communities.

Consider, for instance, the story of Heval Kelli. Heval is a Syrian-American whose family came to the US as refugees about twenty years ago. Heval and his family were part of the despised Kurdish minority in Syria. This is a population that had long experienced discrimination and persecution. However, it wasn't until Syria's secret police arrested, tortured, and three months later released Heval's dad that the family decided to flee the situation.

The journey to the US was a long and difficult one. Granted refugee status, the Kellis waited five long years before they were settled in their new home, the US. Shortly after they arrived, the health of Heval's parents began to deteriorate. The physical and emotional effects of persecution had taken their toll. Eighteen-year-old Heval knew he needed to step up and help out the family. As a result, he got a job washing dishes at a local restaurant. After graduating from high school with straight A's, Heval went on to college. There he completed a degree in premed while continuing to wash dishes and do other jobs to support his family.

Heval went on to medical school, specializing in cardiology. He became one of the first Kurdish-American cardiologists in the US. In addition to his work as a cardiologist, Heval volunteers at a free health clinic that primarily serves immigrants, and more particularly, refugees. Because of his own journey, Heval quickly recognizes the symptoms and needs of his patients and works effectively to establish a plan to promote their healing and health.

Heval has also established several mentoring programs. The Young Physicians Initiative, for instance, is a program that inspires young people in underserved communities to pursue careers in medicine and helps them achieve that goal. As a dishwasher become doctor, Heval has devoted his life and his talents to giving back to the country and its citizens who made life possible for him and his family.

Myth #3:
Immigrants take jobs away from
American workers.

While this is a common perception, the truth is quite the opposite. Immigrants start businesses at twice the rate of native-born individuals. Because of this, they are more likely to create jobs and contribute to the economy than take away from it. In fact, states with large numbers of immigrants report lower unemployment rates for everyone.

Furthermore, rather than competing for jobs, research shows that native-born persons and immigrants tend to work in sectors that complement each other. For instance, immigrant workers make up 30% of the construction workforce, an industry which has significant labor shortages. Because their employment increases housing construction, all the supporting industries for construction (contractors, electricians, plumbers, as well as manufacturers of appliances, etc.) also have a higher demand for workers.

CULTURE-MAKING AND CULTURE-SHARING

Each human being has gifts and talents they can use to bless and enrich the lives of those around them. This potential of human beings to be a blessing to the world is true not just individually, however, but also collectively. People of common descent practice culture-making through the production of customs, traditions, values, and beliefs. These shared notions about the world find expression in language, art, music, dance, science, technology, food, and social structures. Through culture-making, we represent God's creative Spirit in us. This is another way we live out the commission given to all human beings to fill the earth and care for it.

Scripture, however, doesn't imagine that each person and each community will develop culture just for its own benefit. Rather, in Scripture, we see God's vision that our contributions—our culture-making—are something to be shared. We see this in the books of Isaiah and Revelation, for instance. Here the biblical authors articulate God's vision for a community in which every tongue, tribe, and nation will gather together to worship the Lord (Isaiah 2:1–4; 14:1; Revelation 7:9; cf. Ezekiel 47:21–23). In this community, cultural differences are not denied or downplayed. Rather, the image we see is that of all nations bringing before God the very best of their culture's developments and contributions (Revelation 21:24–26). In this vision, the biblical writers show us something of what it means to honor the image of God in others. We honor others by welcoming, creating space for, and celebrating what is good in their culture-making and cultural contributions.

This is not to say that all culture-making or expressions of culture are virtuous. Sin has infected all parts of our world so that every culture has in it good and bad. This is just as true of American culture as it is of the cultures of other nations. As such, the affirmation and the celebration of cultural contributions come with the task of discerning what is truly good and beautiful and God-honoring.

Even with this recognition, however, the biblical writers affirm that cultural difference in and of itself is not bad. The kingdom of God will be made up of people from every tribe and tongue. Our cultural contributions will be purified, not discarded. Because of this, even in the here and now, we can celebrate and receive with gratitude the unique offerings of those from different cultures.

Paul reflects this sentiment in 1 Corinthians 12 when he talks about the body of Christ being made up of many parts. Each person, whether Jew or Greek, slave or free, has a role to play in building up the body (v. 13). In the contributions of the different parts of the body, there is mutual blessing. The sense we get from Scripture, then, is that people of other cultures don't threaten our own. Instead, the sharing of cultural gifts strengthens and enhances the human community as a whole.

THE CHALLENGE AND BLESSING OF CROSS-CULTURAL RELATIONSHIPS

Of course, anyone who has had close relationships with those from other cultures knows that this vision is not easy. Living in community with people who have different customs, traditions, and values will not always be comfortable. Culture clash is real, and learning to communicate well and to work through areas of difference requires a tremendous amount of maturity, patience, and willingness to compromise. Furthermore, we are all more naturally drawn to and at home with our own traditions, customs, and values. Creating space for and opening oneself up to embrace the cultural contributions of others can be a difficult and at times humbling process.

Throughout the book of Acts, we see the early church struggling with this very issue. How can Jews and Gentiles become one community united in their worship of God when they are culturally so different? The Bible suggests that the cross of Christ and the power of the Spirit make this possible.

Consider, for instance, the story of Peter and Cornelius in Acts 10. As was the conviction among the Jews of his day, Peter believed that it was wrong for a Jew to associate or visit with Gentiles (v. 28). Gentiles were considered unclean. However, God showed Peter through a vision that he should not treat as unclean what God has made pure. This was not an easy lesson for Peter, to be sure. Peter thought his own holiness and righteousness depended on keeping himself separate from those of other cultures.

Throughout the Gospels and in this story in Acts, however, we see Jesus and the Spirit teaching Peter that association with those of other cultures does not make him unclean but what is inside him, what comes from his heart is unclean (Matthew 15:18–20). At the end of his encounter with Cornelius and his family, Peter confesses, "I really am learning that God doesn't show partiality to one group of people over another. Rather, in every nation, whoever worships him and does what is right is acceptable to him" (Acts 10:34–35).

When Peter returned to the believers in Jerusalem after his visit with Cornelius, they were upset. They didn't like that Gentiles were being welcomed into the church. But the Holy Spirit opened their hearts to see how God was making a way for Gentiles to be part of the family of God (Acts 11:18). In the early church, through the power of the Spirit, God broke down the barrier of hatred that divided the Jews and the Gentiles. Because of this, the gospel went out to all the nations. We now are the beneficiaries of this, for on account of the early Jewish converts welcoming Gentile believers into the body of Christ, the gospel has come to us as well.

Sin continues to tear apart the human community, foregrounding difference rather than similarity. Instead of seeing one another as fellow human beings who have something of value to contribute to this world, we tend to see those who are different from us as a threat. We live out the story of the Jews and the Gentiles in the early church again and again, communities separated by difference that God longs to join together around the worship of himself.

In this context, our call as Christians is to walk by the Spirit, choosing every day to reject the inclinations and impulses of the old self. When it comes to immigrants, this means bucking current cultural forces that are rooted in fear and hostility toward those from other countries and adopting a posture of welcome, seeking in them the image of God. It means creating space for and receiving with gratitude the contributions they will make to our communities. It means trusting that, in the end, God's vision for the world really is better than our own.

Immigrants and Vulnerability

4

There is nothing easy about leaving behind everything and everyone you know and moving to a new country. Even under the best of circumstances, with a work visa in hand or the sponsorship of a family member, such a move takes a significant amount of courage, inner strength, and willpower. It is true that in immigrating, immigrants gain a new home with all the opportunities and pleasures that the country of destination affords. But immigrants also incur a tremendous amount of loss. They give up the comfort of supportive networks of family and friends, familiarity with language and customs, social standing in a community, not to mention a sense of belonging and of being known. Because the psychological and emotional challenges are so significant, few embark on this journey out of sheer adventure, and many would prefer to stay in their country of origin if life was possible there.

Unfortunately, for many immigrants, staying in their homeland is not a viable option. Violence, persecution, war, poverty, political instability, food shortages as a result of climate change, and ethnic or religious discrimination cause many to flee their communities. Embarking on a dangerous journey, they head toward a new country to claim asylum. Along the way, they are vulnerable to theft, rape, kidnapping and trafficking, abuse, exposure to the elements, starvation, and murder. For this reason, many choose to travel with a caravan for the support and protection it offers for the journey.

LIFE AT THE SOUTHERN BORDER

Exhausted, traumatized, lonely, and afraid, asylum seekers show up at the southern border of the United States looking for help. What they long for is safety, protection, and a chance at a new life. Currently, however, asylum seekers are greeted with endless waits for entrance into the US, long stays in detention centers where they are separated from their children, and a complex legal system that makes a successful asylum claim extremely difficult. It is especially hard for those trying to navigate the system as non-English speakers.

In April 2018, the government implemented a practice called "metering," which limits the number of asylum seekers who can enter the US on any given day. Asylum seekers receive a number when they arrive at the US border. They must then wait on the Mexican side of the border anywhere between two weeks to four months for their turn to make their asylum claim to US Border Patrol. During this period, asylum seekers must fend for themselves, finding ways to provide for their basic needs until their number is called. At border towns, asylum seekers often live in squalid conditions for months, vulnerable to disease, hunger, violence, and discrimination.

Some have noted that the current system is not designed to welcome and protect asylum seekers but rather to incarcerate and deport them. Those who come to the southern border of the US quickly discover that ports of entry are significantly under-resourced to handle the numbers of those who seek to cross into the country.

Out of desperation, some abandon the ports of entry and choose instead the dangerous alternative of crossing the hot, dry desert and the unpredictable waters of the Rio Grande. The goal for such asylum seekers is to cross over into the US and then turn themselves in to Border Patrol on the US side. Not all succeed in completing the journey. According to US Customs and Border Protection, in the last twenty-five years, over 7,800 people have died trying to make this journey. Organizations like Border Angels, which work among and minister to immigrants, believe the number of deaths is closer to 11,000.

What is evident is that to be an asylum seeker is to be in a position of extreme vulnerability. Asylum seekers are vulnerable to the effects of corruption, violence, and poverty in their country of origin. They are vulnerable to exploitation and abuse in their journey to find a new home. They are vulnerable to the whims of government officials in their country of destination. And they are vulnerable to discrimination, racism, injustice, and oppression in their new home. Survival, for many asylum seekers, is largely dependent on the goodwill of others.

AN ASYLUM SEEKER'S JOURNEY

This vulnerability is reflected clearly in the story of Mayra and her children. Mayra, a young widow, fled with her three children from their Honduran home after gangs murdered her brothers, sister, and pastor. As they were making their way toward the US border, they were captured by traffickers who robbed them and held them hostage. In their captors' home, they slept on dirty mattresses surrounded by noise, drugs, and sexual violence. It wasn't long before the kidnappers began grooming Mayra's preteen daughter for sex. Mayra was terrified but knew she had to get out of there. As Mayra herself testifies, God sustained her in that moment and gave her courage. She got up, grabbed her kids, escaped the house, and continued north toward the US.

Once Mayra and her children arrived at the border, they were held at an icy processing center awaiting news of their fate. Because it was determined that they had a credible claim to asylum, they were allowed into the country. After receiving a court date for an asylum hearing, Mayra and her children were released onto the streets of a small town in Texas, left to fend for themselves. By the grace of God, a missionary found them and sent them to a mission for immigrants in San Antonio, where they were welcomed with fresh sheets, a warm bath, food, and even toys.

Mayra's story is horrifying. Still, she counts herself among the blessed ones who made it to the US and have been allowed in—at least for now. Many others never make it to the border or die trying. Still others congregate in Mexican border towns in makeshift dwellings with little access to basic necessities while they wait for months for their number to be called. Among those who flee, there is little illusion about the dangers that lie ahead of them. But for so many, staying in their homeland is no longer an option.

Myth #4:
Immigrants are a burden on the social systems of the US.

This is a common misperception. However, most studies show that immigrants pay more taxes than they receive in benefits.

This is especially true of undocumented immigrants who contribute about $11.6 billion in taxes to state and local governments through income, sales, and property taxes. However, because they are undocumented, they are not eligible for most social benefits like Medicaid, Medicare, SSI disability, social security payments, and food stamps.

CONCERN FOR IMMIGRANTS IN THE OLD TESTAMENT

The vulnerability that immigrants experience today was the case also in the ancient world. For this reason, the Bible includes immigrants among other vulnerable populations such as the widow, the orphan, and the poor, to whom Israel was to give special attention and care. According to

the law and the prophets in the Old Testament, this attention and care was not optional but rather a fundamental
expression of what it meant to live as God's people. For
this reason, concern for the immigrant was incorporated
into Israel's law. By God's command, Israel was to treat
immigrants justly, fairly, in the same way they would treat
one of their own. Furthermore, Israel was to provide for
the basic human needs of immigrants when they weren't
able to provide for themselves. Even a small sampling of
texts from the Old Testament law codes reveals this concern and care for the immigrant.

> When immigrants live in your land with you, you
> must not cheat them. Any immigrant who lives with
> you must be treated as if they were one of your cit-
> izens. You must love them as yourself, because you
> were immigrants in the land of Egypt. (Leviticus
> 19:33-34; also Exodus 22:21; Deuteronomy 27:19)

> Do your work in six days. But on the seventh day
> you should rest so that your ox and donkey may
> rest, and even the child of your female slave and
> the immigrant may be refreshed. (Exodus 23:12)

> When you harvest your land's produce, you must
> not harvest all the way to the edge of your field;
> and don't gather up every remaining bit of your
> harvest. Also do not pick your vineyard clean or

gather up all the grapes that have fallen there. Leave these items for the poor and the immigrant; I am the LORD your God. (Leviticus 19:9-10; also Leviticus 23:22; Deuteronomy 24:19-21)

Every third year you must bring the tenth part of your produce from that year and leave it at your city gates. Then the Levites, who have no designated inheritance like you do, along with the immigrants, orphans, and widows who live in your cities, will come and feast until they are full. (Deuteronomy 14:28–29; also Deuteronomy 26:12)

What is evident in these laws is a concern to protect immigrants from potential abuse and discrimination as well as to ensure their well-being. These sentiments are not simply a passing thought in Scripture. Instead, they are found throughout the Torah (the first five books of the Bible), the Psalms (for example, Psalm 146:9), and the Prophets (for example, Jeremiah 7:5–6; Ezekiel 22:29; Zechariah 7:10; Malachi 3:5).

NEW TESTAMENT ATTITUDES TOWARD THE FOREIGNER

When we turn to the Gospels, we see these attitudes toward foreigners embodied in the life of Jesus. Jesus extended love, care, and hospitality to both Jews and non-Jews.

Consider, for instance, Jesus's healing of the Roman centurion's servant (Matthew 8:5–13; Luke 7:1–10) or the Canaanite woman's daughter (Matthew 15:21–28). Note the respect and care Jesus showed to the Samaritan woman at the well (John 4:4–42). In Matthew and Mark, we read that Jesus made it a habit to minister to the mixed crowds of Jews and Gentiles that gathered around him (Matthew 4:23–25; Mark 3:7–8).

As Jesus practiced hospitality to and care for the foreigner in his midst, he exhorted his followers to do the same. In Luke 10, in response to the question "What must I do to gain eternal life?" Jesus answers with the story of the good Samaritan and tells the expert in the law to go and do likewise. He is to care for and show hospitality to even the stranger whose cultural beliefs and practices he doesn't necessarily approve of or like. Later, teaching his disciples about the final judgment, Jesus asserts:

> Then the king will say to those on his right, "Come, you who will receive good things from my Father. Inherit the kingdom that was prepared for you before the world began. I was hungry and you gave me food to eat. I was thirsty and you gave me a drink. I was a stranger and you welcomed me. I was naked and you gave me clothes to wear. I was sick and you took care of me. I was in prison and you visited me." Then those who are righteous will reply to him, "Lord, when did we see you hungry and feed

you, or thirsty and give you a drink? When did we see you as a stranger and welcome you, or naked and give you clothes to wear? When did we see you sick or in prison and visit you?" Then the king will reply to them, "I assure you that when you have done it for one of the least of these brothers and sisters of mine, you have done it for me." (Matthew 25:34–40)

What is clear from these passages is that, for Jesus, how we treat our neighbor, especially vulnerable populations such as foreigners and immigrants, is a measure of our love for God.

Later New Testament texts reiterate these attitudes, similarly identifying hospitality to strangers as an outworking of the gospel in our lives. Paul, for instance, exhorts the Christians in Rome to "contribute to the needs of God's people, and welcome strangers into your home" (Romans 12:13). The author of Hebrews notes, "Let mutual love continue. Do not neglect the love of strangers, for because of this, some have hosted angels unawares" (13:1–2, translation mine). While many Bibles translate this verse as "don't forget to show hospitality to strangers," the Greek word *philoxenia* literally means "love of stranger." Verse 2 is an extension of the command in verse 1. Roughly paraphrased, the two verses read, "Continue loving each other as family [*philadelphia*], and do not neglect to love the stranger [*philoxenia*]." In other words, treat the stranger with the same regard as you would treat a family member.

LOVING THE THINGS GOD LOVES

This attitude of protection of and care for the stranger or the immigrant in ancient Israel's law codes and throughout the rest of Scripture was unique in the ancient Near East. It set God's people apart from the surrounding nations. In other ancient law codes, immigrants were virtually absent, leaving them without protections under the law. But one of the ways the people of Israel were to demonstrate their difference among the nations and reflect the goodness and love of God was in the way they treated the immigrant.

The reasons for this were stated often. First, the Israelites were foreigners in Egypt and knew what it was like to be immigrants. They had experienced for themselves all the vulnerabilities, injustices, and discriminations that come with being strangers in a strange land. They also knew that this was not what God desired for people. Hearing their cries, God delivered this motley crew of oppressed immigrants from the land of Egypt. It was God's welcome and care for them as a people (both physically and spiritually) that ensured their survival. Because of this, the people of God were called to live out his love and care to the rest of the world.

The second reason Israel was to love the immigrant was quite simply because God loves the immigrant.

> The LORD your God is the God of all gods and Lord of all lords, the great, mighty, and awesome God who doesn't play favorites and doesn't take

bribes. He enacts justice for orphans and widows, and he loves immigrants, giving them food and clothing. That means you must also love immigrants because you were immigrants in Egypt. (Deuteronomy 10:17–19)

To love God is to love the things God loves. And as God loves immigrants, so should we. Again and again, the Scriptures show us God's heart for the broken, the lost, the vulnerable, the oppressed, the ones most deeply affected by the sin and evil in this world. Again and again, they testify to a God who seeks to redeem and restore this world, overturning systems and practices and hearts that perpetuate human suffering. Again and again, the Scriptures tell us of a God who seeks to bring healing and shalom to all peoples and nations. And again and again, they testify to a God who invites his people to be part of this redemptive work, to join with God in making all things new.

The challenges of immigration are complex. There are many considerations and perspectives that need to be weighed against one another. Today, however, many of the voices weighing in on the conversation are quite negative about immigrants. Nationalism is running high, and attitudes of protectionism are dominating the discourse. Amid this cacophony of voices and opinions, the questions Christians need to ask are What posture will we take? What voice will we contribute? What is a faith-filled response to the global refugee crisis?

When we consider the issue of immigration from a posture of faith, one thing that certainly stands out is that God has a heart for the vulnerable. He sees their suffering and commands his people to act in ways that promote justice and compassion. Whatever our contribution to this conversation will be, then, it ought to be characterized by justice and compassion. Our attitude toward immigrants ought to reflect the mind of Christ. In this sense, as Christians we must think beyond what we think is best for us or for the United States to consider what is best for all those whom God loves.

Undocumented Immigrants and Romans 13

5

For some Christians, the main concern with respect to immigration is with those who enter the country illegally. What are we to think about those who cross the border without authorization? Aren't they breaking the law? Shouldn't they get in line like everyone else?

This is a real concern and one that Christians cannot take lightly. Romans 13:1–2 is clear in its exhortation to submit to governing authorities.

> Every person should place themselves under the authority of the government. There isn't any authority unless it comes from God, and the authorities that are there have been put in place by God. So anyone who opposes the authority is standing against what God has established. People who take this kind of stand will get punished.

Generally, we ought not take the law into our own hands. But we miss the point here if we think these verses are a call to uncritical obedience to government authorities.

THE RISE OF THE CULT OF CAESAR

The fastest-growing religion among the Gentiles during the time of Paul was the worship of Caesar. The Greco-Roman culture was thoroughly polytheistic, with many religions being practiced simultaneously. However, the cult of Caesar was unique in its expansive claims. For instance, it claimed that the emperor had instituted a new world order and had brought justice, peace, and salvation to the Roman Empire. The emperor was the lord (*kyrios*), to whom his subjects throughout the empire claimed allegiance.

These expansive claims positioned the cult of Caesar in direct conflict with and opposition to the claims of Christianity. Throughout the book of Romans, Paul challenges these claims in order to set the record straight and to encourage the Christians in Rome in their faith. Not Caesar but Jesus is Lord, he insists. It is Jesus whom we worship. It is Jesus in whom we have salvation. For Paul, Caesar may be on the throne, but Jesus is the world's rightful ruler.

LIVING FOR JESUS IN THE CONTEXT OF THE EMPIRE

The question, then, is How does one live out their faith in this context? How does one wait patiently for the Lord's return in a political climate that is increasingly at odds with what one believes? What does it look like to be a Christian under the reign of Caesar while waiting for the day when all will recognize Jesus as Lord?

This is the matter Paul seems to be addressing in Romans 12–15. According to Paul, Christians are called to live out the values of the kingdom of God here and now. "Don't be conformed to the patterns of this world," Paul writes, "but be transformed by the renewing of your minds so that you can figure out what God's will is" (Romans 12:2). Paul goes on to say, "Hate evil, and hold on to what is good. . . . Love each other like the members of your family. . . . Contribute to the needs of God's people, and welcome strangers into your home. . . . Consider everyone as equal, and don't think that you're better than anyone else. . . . To the best of your ability, live at peace with all people. . . . Don't be defeated by evil, but defeat evil with good" (from vv. 9–21). While these were not values promoted by the Roman Empire, Paul exhorts the Christians in Rome to set themselves apart from the dominant culture by living this way.

Romans 13 continues Paul's instructions to the Christians in Rome. At first glance, these verses are quite puzzling. In chapter upon chapter, Paul challenges, albeit subtly, the claims of the cult of Caesar and champions Jesus Christ as Lord. Why would he now tell the Christians to submit to the governing authorities who serve to establish and bolster Caesar's reign? One possibility is that Paul wants to be clear that he is not trying to start a rebellion against Rome. The kingdom of God will come but not through revolution. Christianity is a religion of peace, not chaos or disorder or violence.

Furthermore, disobeying government authorities would draw negative attention to the marginalized Christian population. It would make them an easy target for persecution.

Thus, Paul encourages these early Christians to live in peace with everyone, including their enemies (Romans 12:14). Submitting to governing authorities is an extension of the call in Romans 12 to love, respect, and bless all people.

Even as Paul says this, however, he is quick to remind the church that Caesar is not who he claims to be. He is not god; rather, he is accountable to God, and his rule is subordinate to the reign of God. Caesar is a human ruler whose governance over the Roman Empire is temporary, limited, and fallible.

Read this way, Romans 13 is hardly a blanket endorsement of civil government. Instead, it is a helpful framework that puts the governing authorities in their proper place within a Christian worldview. Civil authorities play an important role insofar as they keep the peace and ensure order and justice. But their authority does not come from themselves. It is not a result of their own greatness. Nor does having such authority mean that everything they do is good and right. Rather, civil governments have authority because, though flawed and fallible, God permits them to have authority for a time.

THE HISTORY OF US INVOLVEMENT
IN LATIN AMERICA

So what does this all mean in the conversation about immigrants today? I think we can probably all agree that crossing the border into the United States without the proper documentation and without turning oneself over to Border Patrol to claim asylum is a violation of our country's laws. In other words, undocumented immigrants, in regard to their legal status in the US, have committed a wrong in order to be here.

But even as we note this, we should also note that the US has committed a wrong, or a series of wrongs, that has contributed to the current immigration and refugee crisis. Consider, for instance, the history of US involvement in Latin America.

For over a century, the US has "policed" Latin America, providing military backing to various regimes. In 1954, the CIA conducted a covert operation to overthrow Guatemala's democratically elected president. This led to nearly forty years of civil war, during which over 200,000 Guatemalans were killed or forcibly disappeared. In the 1980s, as the civil war raged on, the US gave military aid to Guatemalan dictator Efrain Rios Montt. Montt's reign was the bloodiest period in Guatemala's history. In 2013, he was convicted of genocide and crimes against humanity for killing over 1,700 indigenous Mayans, raping and torturing countless others, and razing hundreds of Mayan villages.

The US also intervened in El Salvador's civil war in the 1980s. Archbishop Oscar Romero published an open letter to the US government, begging the US to withdraw military aid to the Salvadoran regime because of human rights abuses and massacres on the part of the army. Over the course of the twelve-year civil war under the US-backed military regime, more than 75,000 people, many who were civilians, were killed, and over one million people were displaced. The destabilizing effects of these interventions have played a significant role in the poverty, instability, and violence that now drive people from the region.

Myth #5
Building a wall along our southern border will stop unauthorized immigration.

Actually, a wall along the southern border is not likely to prevent unauthorized immigration. About 42% of undocumented persons are in the country because they overstayed their work, education, or tourist visas, not because they crossed the border illegally.

Additionally, a wall will not stop desperate people. As long as there is poverty, violence, and persecution in other parts of the world, people will continue to find ways to come to the US, no matter how big the wall is.

THE HISTORY OF US IMMIGRATION POLICY

It is also worth noting that US immigration policy has a long history of discriminatory practices, privileging certain ethnic groups over others. In fact, the practice of privileging some over others plays a significant role in explaining how settlers of European descent came to have the upper hand in the Americas. This, after all, was not a land that originally belonged to them. Based on the concept of "discovery," however, European settlers laid claim to the land.

As early as the fifteenth century, European monarchies had been using the Doctrine of Discovery to legitimize the colonization of land outside of Europe. The Doctrine of Discovery granted the right to ownership of land to those who "discovered" it. Thus, whatever land they happened upon, explorers claimed rights to it for the monarchy they served, even when the land was already inhabited. The US continued this policy, using it to justify the seizing of land inhabited by indigenous peoples.

European settlers did not ask permission to come here or try to fit in to the culture of the indigenous peoples. Instead, they simply settled here and, after a while, claimed squatter's rights. It was by deceit and by force, then, that the first Caucasian settlers claimed the right to live here. After a while, they developed laws and policies that preserved their claim to the land and created a social system that ensured their dominance.

Immigration policy that was designed to allow some in and keep others out played an important role in maintaining and bolstering the dominant status of those of European descent. In 1790, for instance, when the US passed its first immigration law, naturalized citizenship was granted to those who had lived in the US for at least two years on the condition that they were of good moral character and that they were white.

From the 1880s to 1943, the US enacted the Chinese

Exclusion Act, banning any new immigration from China. In 1924, Congress passed the National Origins Act, a policy that banned all immigration from Asia. In addition, it blatantly discriminated against immigrants from southern and eastern Europe.

Myth #6:
Our ancestors came to this country legally.
Today's immigrants should too.

Immigration to the US in the late 1800's-early 1900's was a fairly simple process, particularly for European immigrants. Many arrived at a processing center at Ellis Island. There, they were asked about their intentions and prospects in the US. They were sent to a medical examiner. Then, if they were not deemed criminals or carriers of disease, they were free to leave. The entire process took about 3-4 hours.

Today, there is no such pathway to legal US residency or citizenship for many migrants. Legal pathways are limited to those who meet the strict criteria for one of four visas. A migrant must:

1. be eligible for refugee or asylum status;
2. have an employer willing to petition USCIS for an employment visa;
3. be eligible for a family visa; or
4. be granted a diversity visa through a lottery.

Each of these visas come with restrictions, caps, and significant expenses. As a result, they are inaccessible for the majority of those who seek to live and work in the US legally. In other words, there simply is no line for most migrants to join.

During the 1930s, state and local governments conducted mass deportations of persons of Mexican descent. The majority of those deported had been born in the US. A similar tactic was taken with Filipino immigrants. The Philippines, which had been a US colony, became an independent country in 1935. At that time, attempts were made to send Filipinos who had moved to the US in previous years back to the Philippines. In addition, a new annual quota of only fifty Filipino immigrants was instituted.

In 1942, the Bracero Program was created to allow temporary workers from Mexico to enter the US seasonally to work in the agricultural industry. These workers labored on farms, planting and harvesting crops. Though they lived and worked here, these immigrants were not eligible for permanent residency in the US.

Even a cursory overview of the history of US immigration policy suggests that there is more going on here than simply protecting national security. It would seem that our policies in the past were designed to protect the wealth, the influence, and the status of people of European descent. Our present policies seem to follow this pattern.

Finally, it is worth noting that our most recent immigration practices and policies have violated the 1951 UN Refugee Convention mentioned in chapter 3. One obligation of the treaty is that nations are not to impose penalties on refugees who entered illegally in search of asylum if they present themselves without delay. Yet the zero-tolerance policy did exactly that, penalizing asylum seekers by prosecuting them for a criminal offense and separating their children from them.

WE THE PEOPLE

None of this excuses the wrong of crossing a border without permission. However, this overview of US foreign involvement and history of immigration policy highlights what Paul implies in Romans 13. Our governing authorities are limited and fallible. They act in ways that are not always good or right or just. Because of this, we would do well to recognize the injustices we, as a country, have committed throughout our immigration history and how we have contributed to the current humanitarian crisis at our southern border. People are seeking asylum in the US in part because our nation has supported governments in their countries that has made life impossible.

Furthermore, Romans 13 should compel us to examine our current policies and practices with respect to immigrants. Because governments are fallible, there is an ongoing need for assessment and reform of government policy generally and of our immigration system more particularly. Even the quick survey of current immigration policies and practices in chapters 1 and 4 suggests that the system is not working very well. As a nation, we have room to grow in treating immigrants or potential immigrants in more just and humane ways.

Comprehensive Immigration Reform

Almost everyone, regardless of political affiliation, agrees with the need for immigration reform. Our system is outdated and no longer meets the economic needs of the US and the humanitarian needs of the world. What would reform look like? Here are some ideas:

1. Secure the border and make it harder to work here illegally.
2. Revise the criteria for visas to make it easier to enter and work lawfully in the United States.
3. For the well-being of those resettling in a new land, make every effort to keep families together.
4. Create a pathway for those who are currently here undocumented that includes paying a penalty for unlawful entry and submitting to the screening process that all migrants who enter this country undergo.

In the US, we live in a democracy with a Constitution that places responsibility for our nation's actions on "we the people." We have the ability, right, and even responsibility to petition our government when we feel that something is in need of reform. This is our responsibility as citizens. As Christians, we do this from the perspective of our Christian commitments. As such, encouraging civil authorities to act with justice is one of the ways we lean into the values of the kingdom of God in the here and now. Based on our discussion of Romans, my guess is that this is exactly the kind of Christian living Paul was urging among the early Christians. He wanted them to be a force for good within the Roman Empire, living in peace but also championing justice and compassion. This is our calling as well. As Paul says, "Let us not, then, be defeated by evil but defeat evil with good" (Romans 12:21).

Immigrants and the Christian Life

6

Communities of faith have been at the front lines of welcoming immigrants into this country, particularly refugees and asylum seekers. Churches often sponsor refugees by providing basic needs and a support community that helps them get settled in their new surroundings. Many faith communities provide ESL classes and mentoring. Some assist refugees and asylum seekers by helping them find jobs or navigate the health care system. Some even provide legal assistance. The service that church communities and religious organizations provide in this regard is so significant that the government has come to rely on them in the work of settling these new comers to the United States.

THE STORY OF RHEMS
UNITED METHODIST CHURCH

Less recognized is the way that immigrants are helping the church. Consider, for instance, the story of Rhems United Methodist Church in New Bern, North Carolina. In 2004, Rhems United Methodist Church was like many white congregations across the United States: in rapid decline. With just thirty-five aging people in worship on a typical Sunday, the church, it seemed, would inevitably close its doors for good within a few years. Today, however, the congregation is thriving, as each Sunday young families with children fill the pews.

Many of these new attenders are Karen (pronounced Kah-REN) refugees who came to the United States fleeing torture, forced labor, and death at the hands of Burma's military regime. Here they hoped to make a new life for themselves and their families. Little did they know that they would also be bringing new life to the small community at Rhems United Methodist Church.

Their connection to the church began with one member of the congregation, Helen Dawley, who had a passion for and an interest in helping refugees settle in the US. Dawley recruited her church to sponsor two newly arrived refugee families. As she was busy helping them get settled, she decided to invite these families to church. Much to the surprise of the congregation, they came. Not just once or twice. Rather, they made Rhems their church home. Through Dawley's continued involvement with refugee families and at her invitation, more Karen families began to attend the church's worship services. The church slowly grew from an average worship attendance of thirty-five to more than eighty.

Welcoming and embracing these newcomers wasn't always easy. Longtime churchgoers were not prepared for the changes this would make to their community. For instance, though members wanted to have young families in the church, they weren't always excited about the influx of noise and energy that children bring. Some longtime members chose to leave. Others, however, found great joy and fulfillment in the new opportunities to teach Sunday school and mentor teenagers.

Becoming one community took time. At first, long-time members and the new Karen families stayed to themselves, worshiping on different sides of the sanctuary. But the church leadership worked hard to integrate the Karen into the life of the church. In worship services, they started reading Scripture in both Karen and English. In addition, they added Karen-language Bibles to the pews. More significantly, they welcomed the Karen into leadership. Today, those who are foreign-born make up half of the leadership of Rhems United Methodist Church. The effect of these changes is unmistakable. Longtime members and Karen families now sit together throughout the church and mingle together afterward.

Myth #7:
The US does not need any more people.

The US birth rate is 1.7 births per woman. Without immigrants, the US population will shrink. The implications of this for the economy would be devastating, causing economic stagnation or contraction. Without a growing workforce, the US will lose its place as a leader in the global economy.

The church has also added new ministries specifically aimed at attending to the needs of refugees. For instance, they started ESL and computer classes. They also added a weekly prayer circle that functions as something of a support group for refugees.

Through its ministry to refugee families, Rhems United Methodist Church has become a thriving congregation with much hope for the future. But more has changed than can be accounted for by their current membership rolls. The congregation has grown spiritually as well, learning firsthand what it means to step out in faith and to trust God. They have gained hard lessons about how to love and support one another, to be a community of faith, to sacrifice and suffer with one another as well as to experience great joy and gratitude in the face of God's care and blessing. All in all, they have learned more about what it means to be the church and how to open themselves up to one another and subsequently to God.

LESSONS IN SOJOURNING

What this church gained through having the Karen people join their congregation is not coincidental. We have much to learn from immigrants about the life of faith. The Bible tells us that, as Christians, our primary citizenship is not on earth but in heaven (Philippians 3:20). We are sojourners, immigrants in this world (Hebrews 11:13; 1Peter 2:11). Our otherness is a fundamental part of being a Christian. We are called to live in this world but not of it, to hold the things of this world loosely, to take our cues for the shape of our living from the kingdom of God, not the kingdom of this world.

This is not easy to do. In fact, throughout Scripture, one of the prophets' main concerns for Israel and one of Paul's chief teachings for the church is about being set apart from the broader culture and living lives that glorify God in this world. As with the church today, enmeshment with the broader culture was a serious temptation for Israel and for the early Christians. In fact, Israel's cardinal sin was that it wanted to be just like the surrounding nations. This pursuit, however, led them away from God. The sad truth in America is that the church has come to look much like the larger culture, with few distinctions that reflect our having been made new in Christ. Instead of being ambassadors of God's reconciling love, working to influence culture in positive ways, we have largely accommodated to the way things are, becoming blind and numb to the systemic injustices that plague our society and our churches.

This is where immigrants are especially helpful and have much to teach us about Christian discipleship. They know what it is to hold the things of this world lightly, including the privileges that come with earthly citizenship. They know what it is to live on the margins of a community rather than at the center. They know how to cultivate their primary identity while living in a place where they are not part of the majority culture. They know something about sacrifice and suffering, injustice and oppression. And for the many immigrants who are religious, they know about trusting in a higher power and about gratitude to the divine for providing for their daily needs. These are all things that are important aspects of what it means to follow Jesus.

LESSONS FROM SOJOURNERS

Moreover, the presence of immigrants in our congregations can help revitalize the church in other ways. Because their experiences and cultures differ from our own, they read Scripture with different concerns, questions, and insights than we do. We all read Scripture through a set of lenses conditioned by our social location, our culture, and our personal experiences. These lenses both enable our ability to connect with the stories of Scripture and limit what we see. By reading with those who are different from us, our eyes are opened to more of what God wants to teach us through his Word. The attention of Latino readers of Scripture to God's special care for the poor, for instance, has led to new insights into the expansiveness of God's redemptive work and deepened our understanding of the gospel.

Furthermore, while Western culture tends to be individualistic, privileging the individual above the community, other cultures are more community-oriented in ways that are similar to the culture of the Bible. In community-oriented cultures, people look out for the needs of others and are concerned about their well-being. They invest in others, support others, and prioritize relationships with others because they know that it is the community that gives them a sense of identity, strength, and security.

These qualities are reflected tangibly in the practice of hospitality. In community-oriented cultures, hospitality tends to be a highly valued moral practice. While the specific actions associated with hospitality vary from culture to culture, in community-oriented cultures there is a natural impulse to welcome others into one's home and attend to their needs. This is often the case regardless of how much or how little one has. Being able to serve others in this way is a sign of mutual respect. The guest is honored to be invited into the home and the life of the host. But the host enjoys the honor of having the guest entrust their basic needs into the host's care.

GOD'S HOSPITALITY TO US

Hospitality is a key part of the Christian life. In fact, one could think of both creation and redemption as God's great acts of hospitality toward his world. When God created the world, he did so out of an overflow of love between the Father, Son, and Holy Spirit, the three persons that make up the Trinity.

But God did not just create and then abandon the world. Instead, God made a commitment to his world to love and care for it. We see this expressed in the way that God communed with human beings, walking among them in the garden in the third chapter of Genesis (vv. 8–9). In inviting the world into relationship with him, the Triune God demonstrated radical hospitality.

When human beings fell into sin, they broke that relationship and spurned the original hospitality God had extended to them. The entire Bible is the story of a God who opens himself up again and again to welcome human beings into relationship. This posture of hospitality toward human beings cost God everything, including the suffering and death of his Son on the cross.

At this point, we may wonder why God did it. Why give up so much when the cost was so high? Scripture simply tells us that it was God's love that motivated this great mission of redemption and reconciliation. God so loved the world that he gave his only Son. One way to think about this is that, for God, being in relationship with human beings and his world is a greater good that having no relationship at all.

When we reflect on the biblical story this way, we can see how God's invitation to relationship is at the heart of the Christian faith. A beautiful expression of God's hospitality in this regard is Communion. In Communion, Christ is the host, inviting all who long to be in relationship with him to come to the table of the Lord. There Christ feeds us, nourishing us with bread and wine, symbols of his body and blood that were given to make that relationship with God possible. When we partake of the elements, then, we are receiving God's generous hospitality toward us. One way in which we demonstrate our gratitude for God's hospitality toward us is by extending hospitality to others.

RECOVERING THE CHRISTIAN DISCIPLINE OF HOSPITALITY

In America today, hospitality is something of a lost art. If we practice hospitality at all, it is in the form of carefully planned dinner parties with close friends or family. For many of us, hospitality feels like an added burden to already full lives. This attitude affects how we approach being both a host and a guest. Opening our home to those we don't know well can feel like a lot of work, and visiting others can feel like an imposition. It is not surprising that we have constructed a society in which we don't need to rely on the hospitality of others. When we travel, for instance, many of us go to restaurants and hotels rather than visiting friends and acquaintances along the way.

In an individualistic culture like that of the United States, hospitality in terms of attending to and caring for others is largely an afterthought. It is something we consider only after our personal needs have been taken care of. In community-oriented cultures, hospitality is part of their DNA. Insofar as immigrants come to us from community-oriented cultures, then, they have much to teach us about living in community with one another and practicing hospitality both in and beyond the community.

It is precisely because of their unique experiences and different cultural values that immigrants have something to teach us about the life of faith and about what it means to love God and our neighbor more fully. While opening ourselves up to relationships with immigrants may be costly and challenging in some ways, we also have much to gain.

STEPPING OUT IN FAITH

We have a mounting crisis at our southern border. Asylum seekers are showing up in numbers that US Customs and Border Protection cannot handle. There is a huge backlog of those who have applied for asylum and await their plea to be processed before a judge. There is a growing number of those living in border towns in Mexico, waiting for their number to be called so they can apply for asylum. And there are more coming. To date, our solution as a nation has been to enact a number of practices and policies that deter and prevent immigrants from coming, to reduce our refugee cap, to ban people of certain nationalities, and to arrest and deport unauthorized immigrants. Our system is clearly broken and can no longer handle the realities and needs of today's immigrant population. More than that, however, our national response seems to be driven by fear rather than by justice mixed with a healthy dose of compassion.

In this context, how will we as Christians respond? What will our voice be in the national conversation about immigrants and immigration? What will our attitude and posture be toward immigrants who have already settled in our communities? What would it look like to act from a posture of faith rather than of fear? How would that change the way we advocate for immigrants, extend love and care to them, and welcome and embrace them in our own communities?

To be sure, the easier way forward is to close our borders and ignore the problem. After all, immigrants will change the cultural and religious landscape of America. They will bring with them different priorities, different challenges, and different ways of shaping life that may conflict with our own. Welcoming into our lives those who are different from us will be stretching and, at times, uncomfortable. But easier is not necessarily more right or more just or more godly. And who knows what joy, what blessing awaits us if we approach immigration in faith? Who knows what marvelous things God may do among us? Who knows? Perhaps something greater, more beautiful will be the result.

Give us the courage, O Lord, to step out in faith.

Notes

Web Resources

Refugee and Immigration Collaborative: https://ri-collaborative.org

Office of Social Justice: http://justice.crcna.org/immigration

Evangelical Immigration Table: http://evangelicalimmigration
table.com

World Relief: https://worldrelief.org/refugees

Catholic Charities USA: https://www.catholiccharitiesusa.org
/our-ministry/immigration-refugee-services/

Bethany Christian Services: https://bethany.org/get-help/refugees

Series Editor's Foreword

7 *Midway along the journey of our life*: The opening verse of
Dante Alighieri, *The Inferno*, trans. Mark Musa (Bloomington:
Indiana University Press, 1995), 19.

8 **"We are always on the road"**: From Calvin's thirty-fourth ser-
mon on Deuteronomy (5:12–14), preached on June 20, 1555
(*Ioannis Calvini Opera quae supersunt Omnia*, ed. Johann-Wil-
helm Baum et al. [Brunsvigae: C. A. Schwetschke et Filium,
1883], 26.291), as quoted in Herman Selderhuis, *John Calvin:
A Pilgrim's Life* (Downers Grove, IL: InterVarsity, 2009), 34.

8 **"a gift of divine kindness"**: From the last chapter of John Calvin, *Institutes of the Christian Religion, 1541 French Edition*,

trans. Elsie Anne McKee (Grand Rapids: Eerdmans, 2009), 704. Titled "Of the Christian Life," the entire chapter is a guide to wise and faithful living in this world.

Chapter 1

15 **This is the largest number of displaced persons:** "Figures at a Glance," UNHCR: The UN Refugee Agency, accessed February 3, 2020, https://www.unhcr.org/en-us/figures-at-a-glance.html.

16 **Another 3.5 million asylum seekers:** "Figures at a Glance," UNHCR: The UN Refugee Agency, accessed February 3, 2020, https://www.unhcr.org/en-us/figures-at-a-glance.html.

17 **Even as the number of people needing a new home:** Muzaffar Chishti, Sarah Pierce, and Laura Plata, "In Upholding Travel Ban, Supreme Court Endorses Presidential Authority While Leaving Door Open for Future Challenges," Migration Policy Institute, June 29, 2018, https://www.migrationpolicy.org/article/upholding-travel-ban-supreme-court-endorses-presidential-authority-while-leaving-door-open.

17 **It set the ceiling for refugee resettlement:** "Fact Sheet: U.S. Refugee Resettlement," National Immigration Forum, January 25, 2019, https://immigrationforum.org/article/fact-sheet-u-s-refugee-resettlement/.

17 **This policy allowed officials to separate children:** "Q&A: Trump Administration's 'Zero-Tolerance' Immigration Policy," Human Rights Watch, August 16, 2018, https://www.hrw.org/news/2018/08/16/qa-trump-administrations-zero-tolerance-immigration-policy#q8/.

17 **Government officials admitted that the goal:** Jasmine Aguilera, "Here's What to Know about the Status of Family Separation at the U.S. Border, Which Isn't Nearly Over," *Time*, October 25, 2019, https://time.com/5678313/trump-administration-family-separation-lawsuits/.

17 **Approximately 5,500 immigrant children were separated from their parents:** Jasmine Aguilera, "Here's What to Know about the Status of Family Separation at the U.S. Border, Which Isn't Nearly Over," *Time*, October 25, 2019, https://time.com/5678313/trump-administration-family-separation-lawsuits/.

17 **Furthermore, since 2018, the government has continued:** Brittany Blizzard and Jeanne Batalova, "Refugees and Asylees in the United States," Migration Policy Institute, June 13, 2019, https://www.migrationpolicy.org/article/refugees-and-asylees-united-states#Refugee_Admission_Ceiling.

17 **Until recently, the US was the world leader:** Jens Manuel Krogstad, "Key Facts about Refugees to the U.S.," Pew Research Center, October 7, 2019, https://www.pewresearch.org/fact-tank/2019/10/07/key-facts-about-refugees-to-the-u-s/.

19 **Among white evangelical Christians:** Hannah Hartig, "Republicans Turn More Negative toward Refugees as Number Admitted to U.S. Plummets," Pew Research Center, May 24, 2018, https://www.pewresearch.org/fact-tank/2018/05/24/republicans-turn-more-negative-toward-refugees-as-number-admitted-to-u-s-plummets/.

20 **Because immigrants are perceived as a danger and a threat:** According to the Public Religion Research Institute 2018 America Values Survey, this fear seems to be more pronounced among white evangelical communities than the population at large. White evangelical Christians consistently reflected less interest and desire to welcome refugees and immigrants into the US and more support for current protectionist policies than the general population. In other words, there is a noticeable correlation between white evangelicalism and negative attitudes toward immigration. Alex Vandermaas-Peeler et al., "Partisan Polarization Dominates Trump Era: Findings from the 2018 American Values Survey," PRRI,

October 29, 2018, https://www.prri.org/research/partisan
-polarization-dominates-trump-era-findings-from-the-2018
-american-values-survey/.

Chapter 1 Text Box

18 This number has seen a sharp decline: John Gramlich,
"19 Striking Findings from 2019," Pew Research Center, December 13, 2019, https://www.pewresearch.org/
fact-tank/2019/12/13/19-striking-findings-from-2019/.

Chapter 2 Text Box

32 In fact, from 1990– 2010: "Myths and Facts About Immigrants and Immigration," ADL, accessed February 5, 2020,
https://www.adl.org/resources/fact-sheets/myths-and-facts
-about-immigrants-and-immigration-en-espanol. See also
Michelangelo Landgrave and Alex Nowrasteh, "Incarcerated
Immigrants in 2016: Their Numbers, Demographics, and
Countries of Origin," CATO Institute, June 4, 2018, https://
www.cato.org/publications/immigration-research-policy-brief
/their-numbers-demographics-countries-origin.

32 Additionally, there is little evidence to suggest: Andrew C.
Forrester et al., "Do Immigrants Import Terrorism?," CATO
Institute, July 31, 2019, https://www.cato.org/publications
/working-paper/do-immigrants-import-terrorism.

Chapter 3

40 Human beings are to be fruitful and multiply: Some scholars have noted that the verb "to rule over" has left the natural
world vulnerable to use and abuse by human beings who seek
to advance their own interests without concern about the
effect on creation. However, if we understand this commission
in the context of divine image bearing, it is clear that human
ruling and subduing of the natural world must reflect God's

own love and care for his creation. We are not free to rule as we please but rather in ways that align with the one whose image we bear. This is clarified in Genesis 2, where human beings are told to care for the earth and to keep it.

42 **In fact, this notion formed the basis:** "Universal Declaration of Human Rights," United Nations, accessed February 5, 2020, https://www.un.org/en/universal-declaration-human-rights/.

42 **We find these policies and practices detailed:** "The 1951 Convention Relating to the Status of Refugees and Its 1967 Protocol," UNHCR: The UN Refugee Agency, accessed February 5, 2020, https://www.unhcr.org/en-us/about-us/background/4ec262df9 /1951-convention-relating-status-refugees-its-1967-protocol .html.

43 **Consider, for instance, the story of Heval Kelli:** Michelle Hiskey, "Healing Hearts, Changing Minds," *Emory University Magazine*, Autumn 2015, https://www.emory.edu/EMORY _MAGAZINE/issues/2015/autumn/features/healing-hearts /index.html.

47 **As such, the affirmation and the celebration:** The process of discernment can be a challenging one. It is so easy to confuse our discomfort with another culture with the notion that it is sinful. For a more thorough discussion of how to receive those of other cultures with both gratitude and awareness, see David I. Smith and Pennylyn Dykstra-Pruim, *Christians and Culture Difference*, Calvin Shorts (Grand Rapids: Calvin University Press, 2016).

48 **Creating space for and opening oneself up:** For an outstanding resource for developing interpersonal cultural intelligence, see Pennylyn Dykstra-Pruim, *Understanding Us and Them: Interpersonal Cultural Intelligence for Community Building* (Grand Rapids: Calvin University Press, 2019).

Chapter 3 Text Box

45 **In fact, states with large numbers of immigrants:** Daniel Griswold, "The Benefits of Immigration: Addressing Key Myths," Mercatus Center, May 23, 2018, https://www.mercatus.org /publications/trade-and-immigration/benefits-immigration -addressing-key-myths.

45 **Because their employment increases housing construction:** Natalia Siniavskaia, "Immigrant Workers in Construction Labor Force," National Association of Home Builders, January 2, 2018, https://www.nahbclassic.org/generic.aspx?sectionID= 734&genericContentID=260375.

Chapter 4

55 **According to US Customs and Border Protection:** "Southwest Border Deaths by Fiscal Year," United States Border Patrol, accessed February 6, 2020, https://www.cbp.gov/sites/default /files/assets/documents/2020-Jan/U.S.%20Border%20Patrol% 20Fiscal%20Year%20Southwest%20Border%20Sector%20 Deaths%20%28FY%201998%20-%20FY%202019%29_0.pdf.

55 **Organizations like Border Angels:** Border Angels, accessed February 6, 2020, https://www.borderangels.org/water-drops.html.

56 **This vulnerability is reflected clearly:** John Garland, "Fleeing North in the Full Armor of God," *Christianity Today*, June 18, 2019, https://www.christianitytoday.com/ct/2019/june-web-only/migrant-san-antonio-border-trauma-therapy.html.

62 **In other ancient law codes:** M. Daniel Carroll R., *Christians at the Border: Immigration, the Church, and the Bible* (Grand Rapids: Brazos Press, 2013), 87–88.

Chapter 4 Text Box

57 **This is especially true of undocumented immigrants:** "Adding Up the Billions in Tax Dollars Paid by Undocumented

Immigrants," American Immigration Council, April 4, 2016, https://www.americanimmigrationcouncil.org/research/adding-billions-tax-dollars-paid-undocumented-immigrants.

Chapter 5

71 **In 2013, he was convicted of genocide and crimes against humanity:** Elizabeth Oglesby, "Guatemalan Coup (1982)" and "Guatemalan Genocide Case," in *Modern Genocide: The Definitive Resource and Document Collection*, vol. 1, ed. Paul R. Bartrop and Steven Leonard Jacobs (Santa Barbara: ABC-CLIO, 2014), 924–26.

71 **Over the course of the twelve-year civil war:** Kate Doyle and Emily Willard, "'Learn from History,' 31st Anniversary of the Assassination of Archbishop Oscar Romero," National Security Archive, March 23, 2011, https://nsarchive2.gwu.edu/NSAEBB/NSAEBB339/index.htm.

72 **The destabilizing effects of these interventions:** For specific examples, see Julian Borger, "Fleeing a Hell the US Helped Create: Why Central Americans Journey North," *Guardian*, December 19, 2018, https://www.theguardian.com/us-news/2018/dec/19/central-america-migrants-us-foreign-policy; and Deirdre Shesgreen, "How US Foreign Policy in Central America May Have Fueled the Migrant Crisis," *USA Today*, December 21, 2018, https://www.usatoday.com/story/news/world/2018/12/21/has-united-states-foreign-policy-central-america-fueled-migrant-crisis-donald-trump/2338489002/.

73 **The US continued this policy:** For a more thorough discussion of the Doctrine of Discovery and its role in American history, see Mark Charles and Soong-Chan Rah, *Unsettling Truths: The Ongoing, Dehumanizing Legacy of the Doctrine of Discovery* (Downers Grove, IL: InterVarsity, 2019).

75 **Even a cursory overview of the history of US immigration policy:** "Immigration History Timeline," accessed February

5, 2020, https://immigrationhistory.org/timeline/. For a more comprehensive survey of immigration history, see William Katerberg, *Immigration Debates in America*, Calvin Shorts (Grand Rapids: Calvin University Press, 2020).

75 **One obligation of the treaty is that nations:** "Article 31" in *Convention and Protocol Relating to the Status of Refugees.* UNHCR: The UN Refugee Agency, accessed March 5, 2020, https://www.unhcr.org/uk/protection/basic/3b66c2aa10 /convention-protocol-relating-status-refugees.html

Chapter 5 Text Boxes

72 **About 42% of undocumented persons:** Robert Warren and Donald Kerwin, "The 2,000 Mile Wall in Search of a Purpose," Center for Migration Studies, 2017, https://cmsny.org /publications/jmhs-visa-overstays-border-wall/.

74 **The entire process took about 3–4 hours:** "Immigration in the Early 1900s," EyeWitness to History, 2000, http://www .eyewitnesstohistory.com/snpim1.htm.

Chapter 6

84 **All in all, they have learned more:** Heather Hahn, "Refugees Revitalize Country Church," UM News, August 25, 2017, https://www.umnews.org/en/news/refugees-revitalize-country -church.

Chapter 6 Text Box

83 **Without a growing workforce:** "The Demographic Threat to America's Jobs Boom," *Wall Street Journal*, December 18, 2019, https://www.wsj.com/articles/the-demographic-threat-to -americas-jobs-boom-11576673115.